LET ♥ REMAIN

Published By:

LetLOVERemain Enterprise

LetLOVEREMAIN?

Let

- To not prevent or forbid
- To give opportunity to or fail to prevent
- To give an unrestrained expression to an emotion of utterance.
- To hurl an object

LOVE

- An intense feeling of deep affection
- The object of attachment, devotion, or admiration.
- Unselfish loyal and benevolent concern for the good of another.
- The above are great however please see "Love's Definition"

Remain

- To be a part not destroyed, taken or used up.
- To stay in the same place or with the person or group.
- To continue unchanged.
- To be something yet to be shown, done, or treated.

LetLOVERemain

Table of Contents

Chapter V: Hope

Vows To Love

Introduction

Relationships can be hard, right? Try being married, that can be even harder, huh? Have you ever wondered why it's so hard? Is it that we as a people are becoming less and less fond of being in monogamous relationships? Is there a lack of love in our hearts? Have we become susceptible to the hurts that we have had to bare? Do we no longer care about Love and what it entails and offers? If I had to do a survey, my bet would be that, "yes" would be the most popular response to all the above questions.

We are drawing further and further away from giving love, receiving love, cherishing love, honoring love, etc. I truly believe that a vicious cycle is taking place and the only way to stop it is by not participating in it, i.e. letting LOVE remain. It's time for a change, and I want to be one of the ones to cause and allow for that change to come.

I have personally experienced being in Love and not feeling loved back. The reasons behind their lack of response towards loving me back was due to their past hurts. The very hurts that I did not cause or have anything to do with. Why? Why is Love always one sided in relationships? Why can't we just Love and be Loved? Why wasn't the Love I gave good enough to overcome the hurts they felt and experienced? Why couldn't she see that I'm different from the rest and that I wasn't going to put her through what she has been through? Why couldn't my vulnerability and commitment prove that I was different? These questions have gone through my head and fueled my passion for what is expressed in this collection.

This book consists of five chapters; the first three chapters tell a story about an experience with love that sums up my experiences with Love and attempting to pursue one woman to become her all in all. The last two chapters sum up the hurts expressed and ultimately provide the solution for any individual who can relate to the emotions I express throughout the first three chapters. In the first chapter "LOVE" I express my Love and intentions for a woman that I desire to marry. I understand any hurt that she may have experienced in the past and I make my declarations to offer true Love to replace all the hurt she may have experienced.

There of course is a lot that is left to the imagination that brings us to the second chapter "Hate" where I express that the Love story I was pursuing has now failed. How could I be treated so badly when all I wanted to do was Love her? This inevitably causes me to hate Love because I'm tired of being in Love and getting hurt. If I wouldn't have had Love, then I wouldn't have been so open and I in turn would have never gotten hurt.

Chapter three "Unforgiveness" further expounds upon my hurt. I express my unwillingness to give in to Love or even forgive the offenses that were imputed upon me. How can I forgive what I didn't cause or even deserve? The unjust circumstances make forgiveness a seemingly impossible choice.

Chapter four "Trust" is a definitive chapter for Love. I define within this chapter what I believe Love is. "But why is the chapter called Trust?" I'm glad you asked. I believe that in order to open back up to Love after being hurt once, twice, three times, or all the way to infinity, trust will be a key factor to start the process. By defining Love purely and not based off what it's not, I believe that it allows for one to see through the cracks and understand that Love is not the one to blame for our hurts. Therefore, you can trust LOVE in it's pure state and let it remain in your heart so the LOVE story you desire can come to fruition.

Chapter five "Hope"; hope for what? Well, whether you are one of the ones who are in a relationship that you wish to reconcile with or not. Keeping hope alive will be essential in either case. If you choose to reconcile, know that you will have to LetLOVERemain, in order to bring forth the change you wish to see within your mate. Know that you have a choice on whether or not you want to continue with that individual. So, if you choose to do so, then, letting Love remain is your best option. If you are one of the ones who are over and done with your situation, then having hope for what Love can bring to you will be essential. Letting Love remain in your heart disallows your hurts to steal your chance for Love again. It keeps you open and willing to receive what you know you deserve. It also destroys the cycle of pain being spread about in the world.

My hope is that as you read these poems, you can relate to my emotions, my hurt, and much more my passion and perspective on Love. I believe that Love is the foundation of a relationship and I also believe that constantly choosing to let it remain is the anchor to allowing it to be able to do so. I also hope that the message within this collection will resonate with all of you, and will aid you to make the choice and commitment to LetLOVERemain from this point on! Letting Love remain is a true commitment and a serious choice that comes with great determination.

It is my pleasure to have each and every one of you reading my very first collection of poems and the first edition of LetLOVERemain! With gratitude in my heart, I open the remainder of this book to you and I pray that you enjoy, understand, connect, and accept the daily choice within your relationship, marriage, situation, or heart to LetLOVERemain!

LETLOVEREMAIN

What does one do when things are not as perfect

As you think they should be and your

Feelings for one another don't seem to be the same?

What do you do when it seems like all you do is argue, fuss,
fight,

And the relationship is filled with pain?

What do you do with the differences that you both have

That drives you both insane?

What about the obstacle of trying to change the very

Things about one another that you so desperately, want
changed?

How much do you bare to prove that you care?

How long do you wait for things to be great?

So, you can finally say that in this relationship

I'm happy, forever in Love and I know that will never change.

What do you do when you know that you know

That you Love the one you are with and showing

Them Love is a feeling from which you cannot refrain?

What if the very Love that you give starts to feel strained

Because of problems within the relationship so things

Inevitably start to change?

What do you do when you feel like you

Love but you don't like?

You kick, you scream, you argue and you fuss

But you don't fight for what's right!

Because deep down inside you're just tired!

You want to leave but you sit tight.

There's so much pain to the point to where no longer can you cry.

You still have feelings but they're not the same.

And towards you, their actions feel disdained.

You try to keep going but none the less,

You just stop..... Mic Drop.

Love is key. Differences are inevitable;

Disagreements will occur, arguments may arise,

But nothing gets better when pain is mixed with pain.

So, so long as you deem it worthwhile.....

Let LOVE Remain!

All days won't be perfect, there may be storms,

There may be droughts, fires to put out, there may be rain.

There may be mountains to climb, valleys, hills and plains.

But, yet and still, Let LOVE Remain!

Love covers a multitude of sins and brings out

The sun in the midst of rain.

It brings comfort in the midst of pain.

Love goes a long way and sometimes is much

Needed in the midst of being wronged.

Now I know that sounds insane, but just know that

The only way to get rid of anger, hurt, evil, wrong doing, malice

And pain, is by Letting LOVE Remain!

You may not always want to or feel like it,

But just know that Love is more than an emotion

Which leaves you vulnerable and open;

It's an action that becomes active and most effective,

In the areas in which it is currently estranged.

If you know that you know that you Love the one you are with,

Then do just that, don't allow any other emotion to be exchanged.

Be committed, have much determination, much courage,

Much hope, much faith, never give up, and most of all

Let LOVE Remain!!

LOVE

May I

I know your experiences in life have caused you to feel

Like love is a distant hope and wish that will never come true.

While I respect your perspective, I also believe that

It was only relevant prior to me, crossing paths with you.

So, clear your mind of all your past hurts and allow

A true man, i.e. me, show you what you're worth.

And I won't automatically assume that I can consume

All your time and do whatever.

So, I'm writing this love letter full of requests for you,

To allow me, to show you better.

May I love you the way you're supposed to be loved?

May I touch you the way you're supposed to be touched?

May I never cheat on you, may I always be loyal?

May I call you my queen, because I consider you to be royal?

May I build an empire with you and exceed financial success?

May I give you my best and from doing so never rest?

May I caress your every curve, may I gently press

Your favorite nerve and give you what you deserve?

May I allow you to be the only one who I'm

Sexing and making love to?

May I show you that every promise I make

And every word I speak, are all true?

May I treat and endear you? May I respect and honor

Your every desire? But just keep in mind,

That doesn't mean I'm a yes man or fear you.

I just intend to give you all the desires of your heart

So, you know…..Baby I hear you.

May I give you all my love and affection?

May I be your protection and make the last man

The last man that ever made you feel the feeling

Of rejection? With one exception and that is that

You show and give me the same.

May I open your door every time you enter the car?

May I make sure you're ok whether near or far?

May I be the type of man that I've always believed myself to
be?

May I give you that opportunity to allow me to prove that to
me?

Not for any credit or recognition, I just want

To know through actions within myself,

That I'm very much capable of loving someone else.

May I rub you from head to toe upon request

And also, just because? May I light candles on a week night

With slow jams going, all so I can make the atmosphere

Conducive for making love?

May I be a gentleman and allow you to get yours first?

May I rehearse with you before I perform?

May I always leave you fulfilled never torn?

Just worn… out from the experiences we just created?

May I keep you elated through laughter, affection, trust,

Good times and full-fledged commitment?

May I allow you to witness what true love feels and looks like?

May I place you on cloud 9? So, you can leave behind your past hurts,

Because with me your love, my love, our love just took flight.

May I love you like I love life?

May I adorn you and lift you up to be the apple of my eye?

May I help you shine with whatever your passion is?

May I be the one whose kids call you Mom?

May I be your peeping Tom simply because I adore your

Body? Because baby that body, that body got me

Thinking of doing things I never would have imagined.

Only through dreams could I fathom,

Havin someone like you, by my side.

Got my eyes opened wide, constantly asking may I, repeatedly like this:
May I hug you the way you're supposed to be hugged?

May I kiss you the way you're supposed to be kissed?

May I always be around, so my presence you'll never miss?

May I reach out to you, every time you cross my mind?

Even if it's all day every day.

In every way, may I prove to you my love and ensure you

That no other man can match or rise above who I am to you?

Laced with truth, placing you, above any other woman,

Because to me your irreplaceable.

And I know the seriousness of my requests got you nervous.

But just give me the word and I promise I will

Take care of whatever that nerve is...

Baby I got you, I'll forever be watchful.

Because it's you I want to learn, I wanna know

Your every up, down and turn,

Baby I yearn for you take my requests for what they are

And believe what I say to be real.

Your heart I will never kill, I only want to heal,

Build, protect, respect and make it better.

So, don't ever think these requests will go away;

There here to stay so you can lose your doubts or at least try.

Because I want to be everything to you

and more so baby please,

May I?

Apple of My Eye

I fell in love with you the way I fell in love with life.

Unnoticeably becoming infatuated with it,

I made sure to do more right, than I did wrong,

So I could live life and live long.

It's crazy because I never tried to fall in love with my existence.

I guess as day after day went by, I grew more fond

Of living, it just captured my heart through its persistence.

Presenting new days with consistent characteristics

That will never go away.

Like how the sun shines every day and the sky is always blue.

And even though the weather does change,

If you hop on an airplane and rise above the clouds that

Block the clear skies, you will see my claims are true.

I feel like the changes in weather are similar to a mood change.

And even though the layer that we see depicts

One thang, once again that same sun is shining

Consistently. Not lacking, not missing beats,

Just like you. Because your mood may change

But behind it all, your ways are consistently true.

Your beautiful just like life. Your wonderful

And amazing, it's like gazing at a new sight;

Catching rays from a new light;

Walking down the aisle making you wife;

Making babies; giving new life;

Just so we can create our legacy.

Leaving everything behind, gladly making what's

Yours mine and what's mine yours,

And it's all for the cause of me, choosing you, to

Walk next to me. That is as my queen,

Proudly giving recognition that I am a king

And our family is our kingdom.

We have a pride that we created that makes me proud

Slash elated. Because look what we've done,

Look what we've created.

I'm your lion, you're my lioness.

And, I know my analogies are many, but

The reason I chose to use any is to show that

Whatever I am, you are too, and by

Having you, I am that at its best.

You see lions are the kings of the jungle,

But before considered kings, they must first

Have a kingdom to rule.

So that's where having you and our creations

Becomes so important because being a king

May be singular but it's not effective until what it's over is plural.

Life has so many complexities, to know them all

Takes time. You have to live it, study its natural ways

And be open to understand for the sake of appreciation.

Because through many of life's variations,

You will be able to call some things good and some things bad.

Some things you like and some things you don't,

But one thing you won't do is give up your right

To life, all because of the negative things you've come to attest to.

So, in relations to my queen, just like I can

Handle the good, the bad, and the ugly in life,

For you the same is true. I'll continue to seek you out

Learn, nurture, care and build you up, because

I want to bring out the best you.

Just like I want to create the best life, know the best places

To go, the greatest sights to see, taste the

Best foods to eat, and experience the best adventures life can bring.

All things can be related to how I love you like I love life

You are my rock, my joy, my pleasure, my reason,

My lover and ultimately the apple of my eye.

Loving you this way will bring joy, peace

And a change to your last name because you'll be wife.

In you my love remains, because through various

Things, I can say that I love you, like I love life.

Please Say Yes

I have a question that I want to ask you,

And it's my hope and prayer that you say yes.

Because with this question I want to ask you,

I am promising you these things, with much more but nothing less:
I promise to be faithful, I promise to be true

I promise to be honest… I promise to be the best man for you.

I promise to take care of you, and never

Allow you to be in harm's way.

I promise you will never have to worry;

I will protect you, guide you, and love you,

Each and every day.

I promise to be mindful of you and all your past hurts.

I promise to use that knowledge

To show you much better, so you can see your true worth.

I promise to love you always, for better or for worse.

I promise to take this role very serious,

Always hold my accountability first to God,

And always love you as Christ loved the Church.

I promise that while on bended knee, giving these promises

That they are true and honest and nothing less.

Be sure that you have my love, and that you will have it at its best.
So, will you marry me Ms. Soon to be Fontes?

Please Say Yes!!

In You And Only You

Yes, it's true, I have found a wife in you.

And yes, that's right, that with you,

I want to spend the rest of my life.

And yes, that's correct, that you won my heart

Without breaking a sweat.

And nope, it's no mistake.

For God ordained us to be together

And mistakes are the very things that

God does not make.

So, with my whole heart I write to you this;

I can't wait until it's said,

"You are now pronounced Husband and Wife,

Now your Bride you may kiss!"

Because when that day comes and in that

Very moment, I know my heart will rejoice.

Because from that day forward, the first

Thing I will hear in the morning,

Is the sound of your voice.

And, the first sight I will see is the beauty of my Queen.

Whether awake or still asleep the most important

Part is that you're right next to me.

So, there will be no need for questioning.

No need to wonder where my hands are or have been

Because without any reason at all my hands will be caressing the,

Most essential parts of your body each and every day,

because baby I love you.

And today I'm a better man and I know it's all because of you.

We share a love that is not common to man.

Because you're you and I'm me,

And together WE, stand according to God's plan.

My beautiful Queen, my soon to be wife.

I'm so glad you said yes and I'm so glad

That it's with you, I will share my life.

You're an amazing woman and I'm glad

That with you I am in love.

God done showed out, I guess Him giving me you,

Was Him doing exceedingly, abundantly above.

So yes, all this I say is correct and very much true

Please always know and be assured that I have found a wife

In You and Only You!

HURT

GONE

Happily ever after, forever and always

Nobody else but you, it's just me and you,

For the rest of our days. Till death do us part,

Our vows are where it starts,

A short time after is where it ends.... What happened?

Is this the time to start laughing?

Because this must be a joke.

You can't really be leaving me for good?

You're coming back home right?.... No!

That's where my heart dropped.

Matter of fact it felt more like my heart stopped....

She's gone!

And I'm here alone, thinking of all the things

I may have possibly done wrong.

Contemplating on how my wrongs can be corrected.

But when I made my attempts,

It appeared as if they were exempt.

Every effort that I made just got rejected.

How can this be? It was just you and me,

Me and you, we even had some good times

Right before you told me you were through.

I don't know if you understand,

I just wanted to be your man and help

Lead you through this life.

I wanted to always be your husband and always

Have you as my wife.

But that's life, it happens, at least that's what most say.

Don't be angry because you will one day be ok.

Well, that one-day ain't today!

Please someone tell me how to deal with the agony

And pain of wanting love to remain.

Trying as hard as you can to ensure it,

Making your share of mistakes, but

Still willing to do whatever it takes, but

It ends up that there's no cure, its terminal.

That means that nothing else can be done,

To fix or repair where we are.

So far gone, that no right can fix wrong.

And no love can rise above to the occasion,

Because the rising of occasion requires two.

Yes, the willingness of me and the willingness of you.

My heart was still there but yours was afar.

Love o' love please tell me where you are,

Her heart no longer bears the love for me

That's needed in this very moment.

Because in this very moment... she's going, going, going,

Gone!

NEVER THE ONE

Now, I'm not the insecure type who wonders

Whether or not I'm good for you.

For me, it's a no brainer, I'm good for you and

That's just true.

But for you, it doesn't seem you know that to be so,

You never try to keep me, and at

Any given time, with no problem at all, you

Would always let me go.

Even if I had a fresh cut, hair lined up like no other.

Even if I'm dead fresh, smelling good, money right,

All things covered.

Even while being the perfect gentleman, nothing lacking,

Nothing missed and nothing undone.

It still wouldn't be good enough,

Because for you, I'm just never the one.

Never the one that you fully desire.

Never the one to whom you want to fully commit.

Never the one to receive your all, because

When things become too demanding or hard,

You just quit.

You know, it must've been nice, to have in your life,

Someone like me to be there for you every time

You were too lonely to live life alone.

You would choose me for a moment,

Yet when things stopped going, the way

You wanted them to go, before a real

Effort could be made, you're gone.

You see you can point out minor defects with me,

And say that we broke up because of this or that.

But at the end of the day, I'm just never the one

For you and that's fact.

It wasn't low funds, it wasn't the arguments,

It wasn't the fact that you thought I was

Unhappy with myself.

It was that, you were in love with the

Characteristics I bore, however, you just

Wanted them to come from somebody else.

Therefore, I consider myself as the unchosen one.

I gave my all multiple times, I even had times

When I felt I was done, but I could never be finished.

A crazy image being that that statement has been

Made fun of, but in my choice of using those terms,

I meant it to say that I couldn't fully give up.

I loved you too much to think or care about myself

Enough to make up in my mind, that I'm actually done.

Never the one so just face it and move on.

I've passed the finish line, while being

Blind to the mistreatment and uneven amount

Of love given and received.

My eyes are now open and I realize

That maybe its best that I just leave.

But I can't lie, I still ask the question as to why!?

Why couldn't it be me? What was it

About me that made you hold back so much?

Why was it that my love, my touch, my house,

My time, my stuff, was never enough?

Was it just that you wanted a boy instead of a man,

To bypass the true essence of a love commitment?

I'm tripping, getting all in my feelings cause in

This instance, I feel like there's something I'm missing,

But in all actuality the person whose missing out is you!

We could have had a good thing

But it's cool, you chose to give up and be done!

And, now I know, it's because to you,

I'm just never the one.

WHEN HURT TURNS TO HATE

How does the one that you once loved,

Become the one that you now hate?

And if you can say that you hate them,

Should your love expressed be questioned,

Or up for debate?

Well, what I say is that, the hate expressed

After love's distress, is a hate towards the

Love that was built up, which you still bare

But don't want to.

I want to be able to see you and not want you.

You did me dirty, so you're

No longer worthy of my love…. I hate you.

Constantly negate truth behind the emotions

Of love that I want to have for you, but I can't.

Because you hurt me once so you're bound to do it

Again, so now I must break free and escape you.

Cause if I don't, I won't remain sane.

I'll be that dude that's constantly rude,

Because I want to express good love, but from

Doing so, I must refrain.

Due to the hurt and pain felt, now my chivalry,

Acts of kindness, forms of endearment, romance,

Etc., I must withhold.

And become what most may consider cold, but

If you can open up your mind and understand

Love's design, it's not meant to be mistreated.

It's so open to its good ways that

If reciprocated properly, you will never be able to deplete it.

No one likes to be walked over, pushed to the

Side, with no form of retaliation.

The desire for retaliation creates this war that makes

This hurt transform into hate, which creates fate

For me to tell you, "I don't love you anymore."

So many tears I've cried, wondering how and why

You did this to me.

You said you're done because you wanted peace

But what about me? I feel imprisoned

While you're out free!

Did you ever care? Did you ever love,

And want to give your all to me?

If so, then why would you let this love go?

I swear this just doesn't make sense, you see,

My mind is everywhere,

I don't think you ever cared about an US!

And don't ask how can I say that,

Because at this point in time, there's no trust.

For anything you have to say, just go away

And never come back.

I love you, but I hate you,

I hate that I love you,

Placed no one above you, just so I can

End up like this!.... Shit!

What was I thinking? Matter of fact was I even at all?

I climbed up so high never expecting to fall,

And, why should I? why should anyone

Prepare for a love story's despair?

No one thinks or even cares about the negative

Connotations that they may hear others say.

Nope, not while in love, because while in love,

Those negative connotations are empty.

Not worried about those things, because if in the event we,

Will still make it through.

And though sometimes that's true, it just wasn't the case

For me and you… I should have listened.

Took more time to understand my position in your life

And really determine if I was ready to be your husband,

And if you were ready to be my wife.

So, when asked how can you hate the one you once loved.

Its due to the hurt, the agony, the pain,

The stress, the drain of my energy,

The number of times that you offended me.

The things I dismissed, that I now, begin to see.

The pressure in my heart, the weight on my mind

And the shit that you did that I would have never thunk of…

Man, Fuck Love!

EXPRESSIONS FROM A BROKEN HEART

I'm upset with Love!

Matter of Fact, I'm mad as hell at it!

Because I tried to give myself in the name of it.

But I ended up feeling hurt, abused, like I wanna die,

Like I wanna kill, like I can't breathe, like I'm asthmatic.

Why is Love so hard to be given and received right back?

Why is there always one who seemingly gives more?

Why we can't work out a deal to feature on the same track?

Why is Love so dangerous?

Why is Love so cold?

Why is Love masked behind so much mess?

Shouldn't Love be powerful enough to unleash and unfold?

Shouldn't it be mask off instead of mask on?

I mean what's wrong with you Love?

Why are you always the harder choice?

Is it that society is at such a point,

To where hate, pain, malice, greed, selfishness, &

Mistreatment are the greater forces?

It must be, because the things people do, may derive

From many places, but ultimately, we live in a world

Where people make a whole lot of fucked up choices.

I'm hearing voices in my head, making me

Wonder if I'm better off dead,

Because this pain of living I dread.

I don't want to keep going through all the

Things I'm going through, and all the future

Endeavors with Love, that I might get into.

Maybe I should slow down, cause

I'm probably thinking too much.

My homie told me, "bro take it one day at a time,

no need to feel so rushed."

I'm healing through my decisions to move forward,

No need to feel so crushed.

Many disappointments I've experienced with Love,

I don't know if I could ever go back to it.

It's blown my mind just thinking like, how the fuck,

No why the fuck would you do this!?

I was vulnerable while in you and you let me down!

Left me lonely in my house, when you

Were supposed to always be around!

So now that my heart is broken, there's

No more hoping, I'm full of misfortune,

Heart scorching, yet it's O' so cold!

Especially towards that Love shit,

Man, I swear that shit is O' so old.

You made me naive to the things

That I should have known.

The things that in your absence, I would have been

Strong enough to stand up and avoid

Being treated O' so wrong.

But the fact is, I did and I didn't.

I kept hoping and wishing, thinking things would be different,

If I gave enough of you!

But what I ended up with is a heart filled with the blues!

That means I'm depressed,

Upset, it's like I gave you all my heart willingly,

Only to have it returned scorn, broken, battered,

And bruised, then shoved back in my chest.

Like here you go, take this crap.

Love you dealt me a bad hand,

And I ain't even ask for that.

Plus, I feel like you really disrespected me,

So, I should beat yo ass for that!

No flashing back, I no longer care

About the good times we had.

My mind's ample, I trample on the thoughts

Of positivity. No optimism, I'm pessimistic

About the results of what I'm dealing with.

No good thing in sight, I might

Fly off the handle, I have no handle

On what happens next.

So much anger built up in my heart, I think it's time

I get this off my chest.

If you know what's best,

You'd leave me alone. Satan's in my ear

Instructing me to commit all kinds of wrong.

But I'ma stop there, let you know once more,

That due to the circumstances, I no longer care!

I literally give no fucks as to what happens next!

Love I fucking hate you! You can have this piece of shit heart,

I no longer desire it to beat within my chest!

I'm done!

UNFORGIVENESS

Forgiveness, Forgiveness

Forgiveness, forgiveness, to you I cannot be a witness.

I cannot attest to your truths, believe in your ways,

Follow your paths, because to me, you don't exist.

Your nonexistence, implies my constant

Resistance towards choosing you.

I don't want to, don't care to, don't even

Feel a need to consider doing so.

The person that hurt me, doesn't deserve forgiveness

And it's useless for you to try to change

My mind, so it's probably best you just let it go.

Your place in my life right now is amiss.

Your ways are hit or miss and quite frankly,

I don't feel like taking chances.

I'm tired of the temporary love coming

Around with no desire to be permanent,

As if they were freelancing.

Forgiveness, forgiveness, I can't help but to be

Relentless, to each and every one of your requests,

Desires and wishes, for me to choose you.

Because, the ones I have to forgive, dealt me so much

Agony and pain, that the feeling of agony and pain,

I cannot get through. At least not until I suffer them the same.

I can't move on in life knowing that someone

Hurt me and I don't cause them the same, or a

Similar or worse pain.

You see, it was my grandfather that told me

Not to be a punk, "never allow anyone to hit you

And you don't hit back."

And even though the abuse caused wasn't physical,

I still feel the need to react.

Forgiveness, forgiveness I'm unhappy, I'm bliss less and

I don't think that choosing you is going to fix this.

Especially when the offence was taking place,

Their heart seemed so cold and relentless.

They didn't care about me!

You see, everyone wants the good folks to be godly.

Thinking that we should bear with all

Their oppositions as if we're automatically in the position

To forgive and let go, just so that they now have a clean slate.

Then they turn around and do the same thing or

Something far worse, another day.

Forgiveness, forgiveness,

If I choose you I'm weak!

Tell me how am I the stronger person by

Turning the other cheek?

Do you not see that they hit me? You must be kidding

If you think I'ma let that ride!

I take pride in being the man I am. Always taking

A stand and holding my own, so to allow any form

Of offense towards me ride, needless to say

It would be untrue to me.

You see in society, people off rip create their own

Illusion and depiction of who I am.

And whether good or bad, I could

Care less or give a damn.

But what I refuse to allow is your negative illusions,

Depictions, assumptions, or thoughts to be confirmed

By something I allow or do.

Because, it's so untrue, if you think you can

Play me like a sucka, trust me, you just have no clue.

I'm far from it, I rise above it and my pride is on

Cloud 9.

High up in the sky, ready to come down,

Like damn, it's bout time.

I give respect to any and every person.

But when disrespected, I flip to a different version.

My mind goes on an excursion,

And I just ride with the results.

With high hopes that I can make it home

And not do something crazy.

And I know I'ma have to lose this pride, or at least

dim it down, because I gotta stay alive for my baby.

I really hope you didn't think that you could display me, as

Some form of joke or some kind of toy.

I withdrew all my heart for you,

As if it were a check for you to deposit,

But you held on to it as if it were of no value,

And returned it void.

So, forgive what? The past hurts only to

Create an opportunity for future ones?

Man lol, that means laugh out loud. You must

Be crazy if you think I'm going that route again, I'm done!

Can't do it again, can't bear to feel how I felt.

And I swear this pain cuts so deep, I

Wouldn't wish this upon anyone else.

Forgiveness, forgiveness, please tell me, what is your goal?

What is your mission? Are you trying to be a form

Of intervention, so you can intervene my bad

Intentions to seek out my vengeance?

I took chance after chance

With love, but it was

Broken down, abused and often misused.

I'm sorry forgiveness, at this time, you're the very

Thing I just can't choose.

With that, maybe I win, maybe I lose.

But I'm ready to make that choice,

Because at this point, my heart is too

Hard to let you in.

No Forgiveness, no forgiveness.

I Finally Blame You

This isn't easy for me to say, because for O' so long,

I thought maybe just maybe, there were things that

I was doing, that were O' so wrong.

While I'm not here to make the statement that I'm perfect.

I almost feel like, no fuck it, I feel like

I acted the way I acted because you treated me

As if I wasn't worth shit!

What did you expect from me, when the things you

Were doing were O' so wrong?

Did you feel as if your fucked-up actions

Were prompts, with which, I should just go along?

Yeah, we're all human and yeah, we fall short

But nothing that we do, is done without choice.

So, make no room and give no voice to any

Excuse that you think sounds good and supersedes

The offences you made.

The cards were surely dealt and the

Hand, you surely played.

How could you do the things you did and try

To persuade me to think that I'm partial to blame

For our estrangement?

For a while, you had me there but fuck that!

We failed because you chose and wanted us to!

That was never my request and never my arrangement.

So, now you wonder how I can act the way I do.

Inevitably blaming me for my reactions, not actions,

That are seemingly disturbing, but the whole

Disturbance, is caused by you.

You can't tell me I never loved you because

If I didn't, I wouldn't have put up with all

That I put up with, only to have Christ as our image.

Thinking I could be like Him and that our love

Story was like Him loving the church.

While He was trying to save it, she rejected Him

But ended up falling in love with Him,

Because He loved her first.

For that, I'll take the blame, me taking the chance

I took may seem insane, but for me, it was my

Hope, my purpose, my story, my lane.

No fame, I wasn't doing it for pride or boast.

Out of all of my encounters with other women,

I realized, that I loved her, the most and was willing

To give that part of me that I hoped, would

Provide validation to myself and healing to my bride.

But almost in an instant, I realized that the resentment,

Mistreatment, and abuse that your love brought forth,

Was due to the fact that, we just aren't meant to be.

You see, you never gazed in my eyes

To realize that my words and actions were filled

With truth and not lies.

You always made accusations, but never acted in a way

That gave reason for me to stay but

Needless to say, I still did.

With high hopes to receive first dibs to

The best you, that you can give.

But what I settled for is second, third, fourth, and fifth place

With no time to waste, I was in the race for my life.

Or maybe I should say, I was in the race for my wife.

But I could never catch up to my opponents

Or be able to knock them out.

We had to go to the cards and you judged that

My opponents, i.e. your desires, won the bout.

And while our relationship consisted of one,

There was still us two.

And for the unfortunate circumstances

That led to our ending, I will no longer blame myself.

Because I finally blame you!

Bitter Sweet

It's a bittersweet feeling, when you have to let

Go of someone or something you love.

It's even more of a bittersweet feeling, when you

Get betrayed by the person you thought you could trust.

Only to pick up the broken pieces and blow off the dust

Of a relationship that once, was but can no longer be.

And while one may beg and may plea,

Things can never be the same, because you broke

The trust that you once gained and now I must let go of you

for good. And I would if I could forgive you,

But forgiveness right now is a foreign language.

I don't understand what it means, I can't

Comprehend when someone tells me I should have it.

And quite frankly I think it sounds quite strange, it's

Not what I was hoping to hear or try to figure out.

I hoped to love and be loved, trust and be trusted

I wasn't out for you to get busted.

It was far from my mind to think that you had

Ulterior motives and obligations.

Because based on our conversations, I was the only one for
you.

But come to find out, that was so far from true.

So, now I am forced to move on, from a love that went wrong,

But could have gone right, so long as you participated.

If your side of the deal was upheld,

Then, we most definitely would have made it.

And I hate it, because failure was never the option,

Failure was never the case, but failure became present

Because of various, mistakes.

So, I must ask where does forgiveness come to play

With these thoughts and perspectives in my mind?

Because if I forgive, I feel like I'm pardoning,

And by pardoning, I feel like you get the best part of me.

The consequences never get sought after and then I feel like this was

All done by design. Because you felt I was such

A good person, surely, I could heal quickly,

And never repay you for what you did to me.

I think you knew I would forgive you.

Maybe you figured I would have no choice.

But little did you know, my forgiveness gave no voice

To your exoneration, in all actuation, it was a gift to me.

And got damn its bitter-sweet.

Sound of Forgiveness

Does forgiveness have a voice?

And, if so, how does it sound?

Is it monotone, croaky, high-pitched, brittle, or gruff?

Is it loud enough for people to hear, or is it

Too soft to be heard?

Is forgiveness just a word, or is it a powerful

Expression that mirrors what many believe

has been done for us?

But in that, can you trust enough, to feel good about

Forgiving the one or ones who hurt you so much?

I mean why should you dismiss

Their dismissals to care about you?

You should beat them until their face turns blue!

True, I know that's how you may feel.

Because the level of hatred towards the actions made is

On a level that kills.

Believe me, it's an emotion I can relate to and feel.

The level of hatred that I could possess within my heart,

Believe me you wouldn't want me to start.

But it comes from the fact, that I have such a big heart.

And I can love beyond depths that are known or imagined.

So, it's hard for me to fathom, how love can be mistreated

In the manners in which most, mistreat it.

I can trust, but when my trust is broken,

My choice of communication, will be through

Words that are unspoken.

No laughing, no joking, just fist to the jaw

And jaw broken, or gun in my hand

Bullets flying, wounds open. No coping

With sensible actions, because the hurt and pain

Leads to unforgiveness and overreactions.

Anything opposing to those things, would be far too passive.

For those who hurt others, be prepared to lie one day

In your bed when its below zero and there's no cushion, no covers.

Or be prepared to rot in hell for an eternal sentence

With no bail or way for you to flee.

And it's all because of all the wrong, you constantly did to me.

And by saying me, I use that as if I'm everyone you hurt.

And I know I don't know the sound of forgiveness,

Because vengeance is all I heard.

But, if I step back and think before I react,

Maybe just maybe, I can avoid going down this path.

I know wrath sounds like the best choice,

But listen closely to the voice of forgiveness,

And bear witness to its power to free you.

You may believe you can't change the circumstances through

Forgiveness and if you choose it, the things happened

Will still remain true. So why choose to forgive at all?

So, you can look your offender or offenders in the face

And smile like; "you don't recall all the things

You did to me?"

When the truth is, you've always wanted to remain your natural

Loving self and never live resentfully.

The sound of forgiveness is not an easy sound to hear or make.

And no, it's not fake, it's not silent or soft spoken.

The way to obtain forgiveness, is by hearing

The plea for it within your heart and allowing

It to be chosen, so that you will no longer be broken,

By the things that someone did to you.

By forgiving, you don't dismiss or excuse anything.

You just let go of the offense and the offender.

So that the same vulnerability in good nature that

You showed them, you can once again be open to.

And, hopefully to one who will appreciate you, for you,

And not take advantage. I know forgiveness

Is a hard thing to choose and manage,

But for the sake of your well-being, I would urge you to listen.

Because within yourself, is the sound of forgiveness.

TRUST

Love O' Love

Are you one of the ones who has been hurt by Love,

So much to the point, to where you don't believe in it?

Are you currently to the point, to where regarding Love,

You are just tired of hoping, trying, caring, believing,

You're just over it, like oh well, who cares, no more, you're just finished?

You ever heard that song by Denise Williams titled: "Silly"?

You know, the one that repeatedly requests for Love, to

Stop making a fool of me.

Are you one of the ones who can relate or agree?

Do you believe that while in love,

You had eyes that could not see?

So needless to say, you believe the song that states, "Love is blind".

And furthermore, you may believe that Love takes over your mind.

I mean it must be, because for me, all my experiences with

Love, have brought forth results that I never saw coming.

I gave it over and over again, I let it remain,

Only to feel like at the end of the day, I was a dummy.

I mean what is love in the first place?

And why while in it, I seem to be last place?

As if I'm moving at a slow pace.

When all the while, I feel I'm moving in such a motion,

To where, in comparison to me, there's no race.

I should win with no problem; the trophy should be mine

I work hard at giving love, for me it's a full-time grind,

Or a full-time state of heart and mind.

That is to say that, I feel and choose the love I have and give.

And loving you is not what I want to do every now and then,

I want it embedded in me so much, that it becomes the way I live.

I wanna live to give love and receive it too.

And not all the love I give requires reciprocation,

It's just the love I give you.

Now I know most may disagree and say that love is selfless,

But wouldn't you say that within the confines of a relationship,

that idea of love, is selfish?

It benefits the receiver, but not the one who imputes.

Love can be a selfless act, but when love is also given,

It is as if it were fuel to fire, water to a seed planted,

Food and water to the hungry, minerals and vitamins to the body.

Needless to say, the constant reciprocation of love given,

Is as essential in relationships as one is to two.

Two cannot be two if one does not exist.

One plus zero is always one, so relate that to

A relationship that only has one person giving all,

And you should see how it creates the

Perfect situation for love, to become amiss.

Let's no longer think of love as a one-way street.

Especially within the confines of a relationship;

Because, with the understanding and agreement of being in such,

There is an essential clause that states, "I agree to work to

Give all of me, my time, attention, and efforts to you,

As you must give the same to me."

No matter which side you're on, both sides must be covered

By the two individuals who agree to the relationship they're in.

And if one can't measure up, then it's not all the way

Shameful for the other to stay and be stronger,

To build the love up.

But, if the other doesn't care or bother

To allow love to grow, then know, you are no longer

Required to be stronger and no you're not stuck.

You are ever the more free to determine on whether

Or not, you should give up.

Whether woman or man, make a full effort

To never leave your partner without.

Because, if I am selflessly giving my all to you,

And you are doing the same for me, then we are both

Taken care of, so there should be no room for depression,

Loneliness, hurt, or pain, all of those things should be

Done away with, with a love that fully assures and

Leaves no room for doubt.

So, Love O' Love, come through for me once and for all.

Please be sure that the next person I give you to,

Understands the principles that will be essential

To hold you up so firm, that we will never fall.

I declare that Love will no longer be seen as a foolish act.

I need you to prove to this world that you work and

It's not bad to be in you, have you, or even be where you're at.

Love O' Love.

Lover's & Friends???

Now, what I have to say is not meant to go against

What most believe they have within their mate.

My very disposition comes from this

Position of how I view love and why I think it's great.

I've never understood the whole lover's and friends concept.

Matter of fact, most that I've expressed this to,

Think I'm crazy. But, maybe just maybe, I have a point

And maybe just maybe, I'm correct.

Now I must admit, that friendship and lovers walk

A very thin line.

But, there's something in my mind that tells me,

That, that line cannot be crossed.

You see, when I think friend, I think of the male friends

I have and as a heterosexual male,

I know that our friendship has no path to being anything

Intimate or so affectionate, that we start catching feelings.

There's nothing attractive or appealing to any male

That I do or do not call friend.

So again, I have never been able to comprehend,

The meaning Lover's and friends.

I feel that when something is confined to a definition,

Then within that definition it is confined.

So, if I call a male or female friend, nothing more

Comes to mind.

I partly understand the confusion, or mere illusion of the

Process behind lovers and friends.

But I always question how it starts and where it ends.

All I have ever known with a woman of interest,

Is pursuit and though prior to any title, we may

Have just been chilling, hanging, whatever and

It was cool. I still would never consider us friends,

Because again, all I've known is to pursue.

The process of getting to know someone

Does not mean that y'all are friends. It just means

That if anything becomes of us getting to know one another,

Then getting to know each other, is where it began.

I also separate the definition behind the two with intent.

If intentions behind hanging out, laughing, joking etc. are

To draw closer or open up to one another, to prepare and

Ensure the next level.

Then I'm sorry my friend, once again, you're not friends

You're on a different level.

Especially when that line is crossed through intimacy,

From that point on you're not a friend to me.

We are something much more, but that definition

We don't always have to find.

Because sometimes it ends there and never happens again,

But still I feel, from that point on, the two cannot be friends.

I know many may disagree, because it's against popular belief.

But if you are still open,

I just want to expound on how great, love can be.

While in love you can laugh, joke around, hang out

Talk about any and everything, pretty much

All the things "friends" do but it's just not that.

Lover's can surely interact on all levels.

It doesn't always have to be romance and rose pedals.

Lover's can also relax, chit chat, unwind, clear minds, and

Still be fine as lover's. You don't have to create

Modes of friendship to ensure that the levels

In which y'all interact are different.

Love can be incorporated within a friend.

Love is how a friendship remains and grows stronger,

However, the same is true in a relationship or marriage,

It's just that the bond and love, is a bit stronger.

With a marriage, two become one

And ultimately join their lives together.

However, with friends not so much.

Friends still have their individualities and come

Together often, from time to time, however, just to stay in touch.

What I'm merely trying to express, is that love is essential

In either situation matter of fact, it's the reason

Relationships, marriages and friendship exists.

It's just important to know that they all have their separate parts.

Lover's and friends, well, I do believe in both,

I must admit.

However, within the confines of a marriage or relationship,

I don't believe the two, can coexist.

I believe Love becomes all within the marriage or relationship

And through love, many things come about.

Like complete and total joy, excitement, affection,

Etc., you will from that point on, never be without.

So long as you marry the one that's meant for you,

Because at the end of all the things vowed,

Is the word I do.

Which declares, willingness and understanding

To all things stated.

And to the many that will agree to disagree,

It's cool, but my belief is that Lover's can

Always be lover's in a relationship that

Keeps them elated. No quote on quote friendship

Needs to be created, just a stronger bond through

Love.

Love's Definition

Is love a form of possession or a mere obsession

With the one you have it for?

Furthermore, can love really be explained?

Or is it only capable of being expressed?

Many attempt to explain it and I must say that,

Most explanations were well stated, however,

The question still remains on whether or not they are correct.

Love is what we feel, who we are, what we need,

desire, long for, hope for and believe in.

Many believe that God is Love, well if that's true

Please tell me how many of you, can truly define Him?

The truth is we can't, we express and bear witness

To many of His characteristics, but the full logistics

Of who God is, is only felt, believed, and known by faith.

We can't see Him, yet we know His presence is near,

We can't feel Him, yet when we do,

The way we know it's Him comes from an unknown place.

We can't hear Him, yet we still profess and proclaim

All the things in His name, as if we were the ones He told it to.

So, in light of God being love, I say that,

Love is indefinable. Yet many of its characteristics,

Are identifiable and recognizable, to the truth

That we all bare in our hearts, minds, bodies and souls.

If you believe that you know God more and more through

Relationship, believe that same thing about love.

You can only begin to recognize it, have it, give and

Receive it when you accept, spend time with, and believe it.

Love is a transformation of self into another, to be them,

To be like them, to assimilate to them, to empower them,

Endear them, or simply to just ride or die.

So, I wonder why, love is so distant in many hearts.

What happens to the innocence and love from our
adolescence?

Does it just end right where it starts?

Or are there sparks that come about, when the

Negative comes in contact with the positive,

Or vice versa?

Does love get better or does it get worse

As the years go by?

Constantly wondering why, this feeling we all call love,

Is so hard to embrace.

Love may seem like a hard pill to swallow, because it requires
your

Full commitment, determination, will, and desire

To choose it, when it does and does not stare you directly in
the face.

Love is inevitable to and demands relationship.

That's the only way you can know it and experience its
depths.

Constantly taking steps in it, going deeper and deeper

Until people can feel love when you walk and hear love
through

Your every word and every breath.

Love is a composition of actions, thoughts, feelings, desires,

Hopes and truths.

Love comes through the likes of me and the likes of you.

Which means everyone has it and can give it,

So long as you choose.

Just keep in mind that when you choose to love

You lose to hate, they carry separate

Sets of expressions, that can in no way, shape, or form, relate.

So, to define love, is to confine love

And love cannot be confined.

Love knows no boundaries, there are no limitations, nor
exceptions

It simply exists for us to experience, acknowledge, embrace
and become.

So needless to say, a definition for love,

There isn't one.

Love is a Gun

You ever heard the saying "Love is a gun?"

Well if Love were a gun, which part of the gun would it be?

Would it be the gun in its entirety? Or would it

Be the bullets, the shells, or the trigger?

Would one be able to point it at its target to get

Whatever they want? Or is the picture of

Love being a gun, much bigger?

If love were a gun, when Love shoots, does it

Kill, disable, or injure innocent targets?

Or does it protect the innocent and kill its adversaries

Through explosive force, when it discharges?

Through this perspective, is it safe to say that the carriers

Of love have the ability to choose how love is to be given?

Causing some to use this gun for good and some for evil,

Inadvertently or advertently, causing love's true

Meaning, to be conflicted?

Some abuse love and make it seem as if it

Is meant to be powerful enough,

To do and say anything to you, without the

Reception of any pushback or negative response.

Just a yes always because of how the presence

Of the gun taunts… death?

Like if you say the wrong thing or make one wrong move

That will result to your last… breath.

So, you inevitably become submissive and fall victim

To the requests of your abuser.

Not knowing that the requests you're obliging to,

Are creating the perfect set of circumstances for you, to be a loser.

Believing that beggars cannot be choosers,

But wait, you never asked for this.

And, just because you are giving love and

Strongly want to receive it back, doesn't make you desperate,

It makes you realistic.

Because, within the confines of a relationship,

Love requires for both to receive and give it.

You're now in the type of position

That is causing you to look within yourself,

To find out whether or not the love you are freely and purely giving

To your current lover, really for someone else.

And though you may not be able to help, the fact

That, you are in love with pure intentions,

While the one you are in love with

Carries a different vision and would much rather

Receive full selfless love, affection and attention.

While failing to give in to the fact, that it's

Ever so necessary that they love you back.

Although In this case they seemingly keep love a face,

Only to replace love's true meaning.

Seeming, to much more depict the negative image of a gun.

Shooting and disabling you from ever being able to run

And get away so they can feel in some way,

That they got you wrapped right up under their feet.

They pull out their gun from time to time

So, you can see that it's there.

Hoping it can create the type of fear

That will make you stay.

Because the appearance of this gun makes it seem

As if they, will one day, open up to the love you give

And reciprocate it back.

Although the facts follow their acts,

Because their words spoken counteract, the way

They actually treat you. Flashing their gun

As a way to keep you.

But, things change when love seemingly creates pain.

It builds up a certain level of resistance

To the hurt received on a basis that's consistent.

And to keep you from willingly becoming distant,

when your abuser becomes aware of the change,

They proceed to take aim..... then,

Bang! They speak the words that leave you breathless.

Bang! Their actions have you feeling alone and rejected.

Bang! Your out of breath, you can't catch it.

Bang! They leave a hole in your heart and you're reckless.

Believing, that you were just a checked item on their checklist.

Because, it's no way that they could love you

And create so much hurt and wreckage in your life.

And, it now appears that you will never be alright;

It's your plight, so you got to face it!

You fight, but fear you won't make it!

And lose hope of someone ever entering your life,

to take away the hurt and replace it.

With true love and bring forth a different perspective

To the analogy of love being a gun.

You yearn for someone, to ensure you that the correct way to

Love, in comparison to your experiences, is vice versa.

Because, you couldn't take it if the pain gets any worser.

You need change, you need the cursor

To be placed right in front of the first paragraph

Where your hurt was first written.

Changing the first sentence, to a more

Hopeful insight and vision, of love in the image, of a gun.

Can someone, please rewrite this love story before you lose
hope?

And take that same gun your abuser used to kill you,

Aim it at your own head, then blow, your brains away,

To erase your memories for good.

Someone ought to if they could, intervene and allow

Love to be seen through the perspective of its true meaning,

Before it's all said and done. And again, I ask,

Have you ever heard the saying, "Love is a gun?"

Well, if you choose to depict me as such, then;

I would much rather be known as the bullets, the shells

And the trigger. Because within this analogy,

There is a picture that is much bigger.

I am the gun in its entirety, constantly firing at all

Of my opposing factors. You know the contractors of hate,

That cause many to become estranged to love's name;

But, I/Love, would urge you not to do the same, or go that
route.

Because you have yet to truly experience,

What real love is all about.

Yes, it's true, I was with you all the times you got hurt.

But, for what it's worth, I was still there to protect you.

And though you may feel that I neglect you,

Every time you give me a chance, just wait and hear me out.

I will never leave you nor forsake you, I will never

Hurt or hate you, or allow either to overtake you.

Please know that many falsely depict my image.

Coming close in appearance, but never matching

To who I am, because they suffer from their own

Sets of pain and strife and choose to choose death and not life!

Inevitably spreading their pain and hurt

On the ones who don't deserve it, but they get it anyway.

Because pain knocks on everyone's door, every day.

But please don't believe, that I/Love am the one that creates
it!

Love nurtures and replaces, the hurts and pains

We are all susceptible to. Most have no clue, the wars

I have to fight, to save the lives, of the ones who

Desperately need me.... I am LOVE, my depths are

Well past knee deep, and there's not a battle I can't

Overcome, believe me!

I go to war with those bad intentions, lack of convictions,

Cold hearts, with no sparks to heat it back up.

Just back up, because love don't live here anymore.

I also go to war with hurt, evil, malice and pain.

And when I'm in the hands of the right ones,

I proceed to take aim….. then,

Bang! Bye bye to your anger and aggression.

Bang! Good riddance to your shame and depression.

Bang! No more hurt and rejection.

Bang! All your pains, sufferings & bad experiences

Are dead, no exceptions!

So, make no more thoughts or speeches

Of acceptance toward those negative emotions

That only crept in, to take you off track.

Know that I will protect you,

Keep you safe and forever have your back.

For anyone with bad intentions just go away!

Yes, I/Love am a gun, but I'm definitely not a throw away!

So please don't treat me as such!

And feel as if though you don't need me that much, because
you do!

I am an essential part of life and it is safe to say

That if it weren't for me, there would be no you!

It's quite simple you see, Love created you and

Is within every human being. It's just

That every human being has a choice

And with that choice, it weeds out the number of

Individuals lives in which I can be seen.

But it doesn't take away from who I am and what I mean.

I mean, I make up the very presence of the creator that created you!

So how could one ever believe that I hated you?

Another false accusation, but it was you, that made it true!

Not I, I/Love existed when you didn't and I will

Continue to exist when all stop living! So, take a moment

To set yourself free, in me and never go back to that prison.

Carry a different perspective and vision because I'm here!

Not to create any agony, pain or fear;

But much rather to deplete such, in the hearts of all

Humanity. So, the above will appear inane.

I/Love oppose and create change, only to ensure

That the evil you now see, will one day disappear. But, it's up to you!

Use love to shoot, down the contractors of evil and hate!

Make love great, because we are the ones who possess it,

And though it exists on its own, it's up to us to protect it.

Love's energy is meant to be reflected

And never objected because of how the ones who are

Giving it, choose, to project it.

From this point on, refrain from putting me away.

You've earned your license to carry me everywhere and every day.

So, rightfully choose to do so, and do know that you are

Free and clear from your past hurts and pain.

So, I urge you to let LOVE remain!

And, understand that there is a war going on,

that without love, can never be won.

So, in the right manner and with honor and reverence,

Choose to fight this war until it's all said and done.

Take aim and create change, then, Bang!

Because Love, is your gun!

HOPE

I Wonder

I wonder what it takes to get a good woman

Now days. Maybe if I dress more like a thug.

Maybe if I smoke and drink these killer drugs.

Maybe if I become rude and don't open her door.

Maybe if I smack her around until she

Can't stand it anymore.

Maybe if I talk to her mean and call her

All kind of names.

Maybe if I tell her what she wanna hear

Like Gucci Mane.

Maybe if I cheat, but still claim to love her so.

Maybe a good woman is someone I'll never know.

Maybe if I start to sell drugs or claim to be hood.

Now days it's just too hard for a real man,

To find a real woman, who wants to be treated good.

They say they want this, they say they want that.

They want to go forward but keep going back,

Back to the same type, they say treats them so wrong.

Make some changes in y'all life and just move on!

On to someone better, on to someone true,

On to that man whom God has sent to you.

Don't dwell in the past hurts, just let it all go,

Cause when the right man comes, you will truly know.

I swear, if I could open the eyes of these blind women,

I would show them something real,

And allow them to see how love should really feel.

A good man shouldn't be considered soft or weak.

For I am a strong individual

And only strive to bring joy to her every heartbeat.

A real man serves, protects, provides, honors, adores and

Cherishes the woman he loves.

He builds her up, respects her

And outside of God puts no one before or above.

Let's do things the way God intended them to be done,

For this is the only way a real relationship, can last long.

Relationships should be valued much more,

But instead this generation, along with society, goes with

The opposite of what they truly seek for.

But I won't get discouraged, because soon they will see.

And I so humbly say, that women need a man like me.

Yes, with a humble spirit I speak that of my life.

Not to boast or be cocky, it's just,

In myself and the way I am, I take pride.

So, when someone good and someone true

Comes along and wants to be with you,

Don't turn away and leave them estranged.

You may miss your blessing and it may

Not ever come back again.

So, I guess what I wonder is, if there is a woman

Out there for me. Whose values are strong and ways

Are of God and will honor the stranded cord, braided by three.

Who will love and value me for me

And not for what I have.

A woman who knows that these worldly

Possessions, will not last.

A woman who will be there for me, no matter the trial.

A woman this strong, will have my child.

This woman will have an unconditional love.

She will be the one whom God sent from above.

She will have purity in her heart and in her mind.

And we will walk a path that only God can shine.

I know I must be patient and believe this to be true,

Because whenever I find this woman that I truly seek for,

We will be together forever and our love will last, forever more.

Dear LOVE

Dear LOVE, many have been broken, battered, and bruised.

Yet, still choose to keep you around. Although,

When we lift you up, you let us down; why is that?

There are so many thoughts in my mind that

Question your existence. Many wonder if the things we went

Through, came from you, or just received your permission.

Everyone mentions how powerful you are, but the scars

Left on many hearts, lead many to believe, that

You aren't that powerful after all.

Hope in you has been lost and it comes at a great cost,

To build the hope back up. Hopefully your keeping track of,

All the hearts that are being broken,

All the individuals who are tired of giving LOVE

So, they throw in the towel,

Taking themselves out of the bout.

Heart's now cold, then frozen and tossed

Into iceboxes that will never be thawed.

Too many flawed attempts at LOVE

And it's all because of the individuals who claimed

That they LOVEd me, yet only went through the motions.

Leaving open wounds on my heart, which gave LOVE,

But never received LOVE back.

The reciprocation was lacked and my abuser often

Felt as if they could bypass at any time and comeback,

But that wasn't quite true. So, hopefully you,

Can come through and teach what hasn't been taught,

Bring joy to the distraught, fight the war that needs to be fought,

heal those who have been hurt,

Place false LOVE on do not disturb and with

One relationship at a time, allow heartbreak to be unheard.

Because there is a woman out there whose heart is now shunned,

Cooked way past well done, hard as a rock and soon

To fade away like ashes.

Many can see that she is hurt, confused, lost, torn, broken

And left trying to find answers to the reasons behind

Her mistreatment and rejection.

She once believed that LOVE was her protection

But she's now changed her perspective, seeing how that

Strong feeling of affection led to her biggest heartbreak,

I mean lesson. Her heart was once full of LOVE

But that amount has now lessened.

Feelings of being cursed, no blessings.

Yet it's a blessing that she is still halfway sane.

With all of her might, she is attempting to maintain

Her sanity but she's in danger.

She tries to evade the feelings of LOVE and

Conforms her broken heart into anger, hate, malice and distrust.

She's been hurt badly and far too many times,

So now she walks in disgust towards all men.

Claiming that they are all the same, claiming that she needs change,

But wholeheartedly believing there is no one to provide it.

Another pure heart shattered, and it seemingly never mattered

Whether or not, she would survive this.

Her heart still yearns for LOVE, but its buried deep down inside.

Pride is now the ruler of her heart,

And it refuses to be open, because it refuses to be broken…

Again. All her heart wants to do is win, win, win

No matter what. But she doesn't believe that she can

Do so by falling in LOVE and providing trust,

So, she allows her heart to settle, for lust.

As soon as nuts are bust, the mission is accomplished.

No expectations, affections, forms of commitment,

Or reasons for broken promises. Just getting

What she wants, when she wants it.

Don't have to follow up, she'll let you know when

She's had enough. After all, emotions can't get involved

Because she refuses, to fall in LOVE.

LOVE! Can't you see that a war is at hand

Many are refusing to LOVE, shutting it down,

Completely obliterating the idea of it

And consequently, getting rid of your supply and demand.

Because just like that woman hurting,

Out there hurting, also is a man.

Who can't understand why his heart is broken.

He had been open to the idea of LOVE many times.

Created many rhymes for that special lady who had

His heart. Yet when the light shined on the dark,

He was exposed to truths he couldn't take.

He had been misused, abused, and drained.

Gave up his whole heart and last name

For a family he wanted to create but

Hateful and selfish acts tore his fate and rid it with pain.

And he is now alone, broken and shamed.

Pride became his best friend, because the moment

He allowed pride in, he was never again brokenhearted.

He started being heartless, a complete savage.

He created a habit of having multiple women on his roster.

An imposter of a player because deep down inside

He yearns a savior in the form of a woman who will LOVE

Him wholeheartedly, so he can reciprocate the same.

But in the forefront, he's heartless, a player, a no good

Brother, who will never change.

Confirmation comes out of his mouth but its only

Because he can't allow himself to be vulnerable

To the hurts he believes comes with falling in LOVE.

So, he confirms what's depicted by verbally proclaiming

That he is vindictive, no good, can't LOVE or be LOVEd,

Trust or be trusted, he states and becomes, a complete savage.

No love, he's had it with that thought of it.

His current state of mind is set and there

Ain't no moving past or rising above it…

Somebody help! Because whether man or woman

I'm sure you can identify with having the idea

That you will never LOVE anyone else after your

Heart became broken.

We are doomed amongst each other,

Because within the most intimate form of relationship known,

We refuse, misuse, abuse and become too far gone

to allow LOVE to be chosen as the source

That must remain. It's almost like, when

Problems arise, we refrain from utilizing

The only source that can create change in the midst

Of problems and pain.

So dear LOVE, it is concluded that you have been

Excluded out of many hearts;

But as one who still believes in you,

Can you start with one, two, or three?

Shoot, start with me, to bring your presence

Back to a place of reverence and endearment.

Can you allow LOVE to cast out the fear in

The ones who fear it, because of all they've been through?

Can you teach all men to LOVE women the

Way you intend, for men to?

In vice versa can you do the same for women?

Can you bring us all at attention to learn

How to date properly and to cast out impure motives

And intentions? Every relationship may not workout

But can you teach us how to do without

Breaking each other's hearts?

And most importantly, if hearts are broken,

Can you help guide us to look at you purely?

Let you remain and always be an option

Ready to be chosen for the right person?

Can you create new versions of LOVErs

That are only out to be true LOVErs

To their true LOVEr? Can you uncover the fake?

Can you cause them to separate themselves from the true?

Can you place the understanding in us,

That you exist purely, alone, but it is up to

Us, as humans to properly represent you?

And with that understanding, can you give

Us the strength, willingness and desire to do so?

Because, we do know, that we truly need you

And most truly want you,

Were just hurt, tired, down and need help getting up.

So, please become that crutch that lifts us up,

Restores our hearts, removes our doubts, and becomes our world.

Sincerely:

every boy, every girl, every woman and man,

That's ever been, brokenhearted.

Where There's LOVE There's Hope

Imagine being with someone for so long,

To the point that, being without them you can't foresee.

Imagine loving them so hard to the point that,

In the midst of being treated wrong,

The wrong you can't see.

It doesn't outweigh the love you have, because

The love you have, shows you a better person,

It gives you a different perspective, a different version.

Brighter days, a forever and always,

And hope that leads you to believe that change is on the way.

And what more can you say? The act of love

Is present, so no failure can come into play.

Brighter days are definitely sought.

Negativity you write off, because you know

Better days will come through.

That forever and always us, forever and always

The one for me and me the one for you.

But somehow it all comes to an end,

And that end is hard for you to accept,

Because all you can think about, is the time you put in,

The efforts you gave, the love you had,

And the fact that you now, have nothing left.

You now feel like a fool, you now feel dumb,

Because you are now able to see clearly

All the wrong that was done.

And at some point, you blame this thing called love,

Because it's the most prominent thing to blame.

Because you gave your all and then some

And it was all done, in love's name.

So, you wonder why things didn't change;

You feel like this can't be life, and you're

Being forced to accept this plight.

If you didn't have love, you wouldn't have allowed

The things you did; you compromised this, accepted that,

And ultimately settled for the wrong bid.

It's true when they say hind sight is 20/20.

Because while looking back, you're trying

To find reasons why you loved so hard,

But the truth is you feel dumb, because you clearly don't see any.

So now you must ask the question, "why did I stay

For so long, only to now seem like a joke?"

Well, if I, being LOVE may interject and answer that for you,

The answer is, because where there's LOVE, there's hope.

You see, LOVE provides the type of perspective

That is forever hopeful towards its objective of

Being present in the first place.

LOVE sees no wrong, but it's no fool to know

Of its existence; the goal slash mission is to have

The wrong's existence erased.

Along with hate's, malice's, evil's & pain's

Pretty much all things opposing to LOVE,

LOVE wants to make estranged.

Never feel foolish for hoping for the best within

Whatever love story you were in.

Your eyes worked just fine and so did your mind.

So, if you weren't before, you aren't after,

And you were never: dumb, stupid, foolish or blind.

In the name of love, you just made a full commitment to

Change the wrong you seemingly pushed to the side;

So that through love, you could

Overcome the bad you saw. You hoped it would

Go away and die, not come back,

Just forever be nonexistent.

And the length of time you gave and showed love,

Happened because LOVE knows to be persistent.

You hoped that through its persistence,

It would draw y'all closer not distant.

Well I have a quick disclaimer; if the distance presented

Incessantly derives from the other side, then it's time

For you to accept the distance and give moving forward

full acceptance and recognition.

If love isn't received while being given, then it calls

For a full revision, because within the confines

Of a relationship, love should rotate 360.

Nothing should be missing, in this concept,

LOVE is fully dependent.

LOVE is not soft, LOVE is not weak,

It knows how to fight, it just fights to a different beat.

Instead of hitting back, it turns the other cheek,

So that the anger one had built up,

Will come down and heap the coals from their head

Through a gentle reply.

Instead of exchanging hurt for hurt,

LOVE embraces, nurtures and cures so

That, in the midst of hurt, LOVE can be revived,

And from that healing can derive.

LOVE requires relationship with it and

The one you give it to.

LOVE knows the struggles of its embracing;

So, it protects, covers, and comforts you.

LOVE is an action and emotion that must be chosen;

So, don't be cold, don't be frozen,

In the midst of some tough situations

that may lead you to believe that it's easier

To be hating. But, if you choose to do so,

Please do know, that you add to the bad in the equation.

Try subtracting the hate, the bad, and the ugly,

Just trust me, it will prove you to be the bigger and

Better person who allowed love to rise to the occasion.

The road to choosing love comes with a lack of self,

Because LOVE requires you to become selfless,

For the benefit of someone else.

You may not always see the result of doing so in

Every situation, but in relations to relationships and marriages…

It should be give and receive, receive and give, the type of

Reciprocation that never ends. Just a constant

Perspective that never falls through the cracks,

And prevents and stops, right in the tracks, the birth

Of negative emotions like a contraceptive.

The two working towards love, should honor fully,

First their commitment to LOVE and second to each other.

There should be no need to look any further,

Because everything needed will be covered within

The LOVE you persistently show one another.

And to those who feel like, love is a no go so you'll just stop,

Just know that the deterring factors came from the

Ones you have chosen to LOVE, while you were ready,

Willing and committed, but they were not.

Don't allow the one or ones you showed LOVE to,

Steal that precious gift within you.

Just as you hoped for the best within them,

Hope for the best within you.

LOVE is what allowed you to stay for better or worse.

And, no, you're not cursed, it's just that time may be

The only factor for you to receive the LOVE you deserve.

So, wait on it and know that no one can drain

All your LOVE, because LOVE is everlasting.

And, if anyone ever inquires or begins asking,

How you can be open to LOVE again,

After all you've been through.

Just tell them, "LOVE gave me hope and if you

Let it remain, then it will do the same for you."

Always remain true, to yourself, if LOVE is in you,

Then accept your life sentence and bid hate a good riddance.

Pain is for everybody, with it we must all learn to cope,

But within that same thing, there's LOVE that can be found,

And within that LOVE, there's hope.

Pain is For Everybody

Pain is for everybody. And, it comes in every aspect of life.

Pain comes if you have a husband and

Pain comes if you have a wife.

Pain comes, whether you are a quote on quote sinner,

Or if you have given your life to Christ.

Pain can be felt in the smallest of circumstances,

To the most extreme. I say this again,

"Pain is for everybody! Yes, every human being."

Pain is the one thing that causes so many reactions

And emotions. Pain causes: tears, resentment,

Disrespect, lack of commitment, dependence,

And sometimes even the lack of a desire, for living.

Pain causes heartaches, pain causes death,

Suicide, depression, insanity, and sometimes the lack to

Withstand any, good deed, there's no need,

Because pain will come either way.

So why care about what I do and what I say?

There's no way for me to escape this,

So, I might as well hate this…. Life!

Filled with pain, filled with strife.

Pain is that one thing that causes a cycle

That is vicious, possibly epidemic and when

Embraced in the wrong manner, will lead to a dead-end road.

Pain can truly justify one's decision to

activate their quote on quote savage mode,

To where they literally couldn't care less

About what happens next.

Imagine, gently knocking on a door to be let in a room

And you know someone is on the other side.

Yet, they refuse to oblige to your gentle

Request to let you in, so with a little more force,

You knock again.

Yet, on your second attempt, they still refuse to let you in

And now you begin to verbally inquire

On their desire to open the door, but there's no reply.

So, again you try and your knocking and verbal

Requests now coincide and sadly but true

For the third time, you are denied.

So now your next response, is to beat down

The door at once, because you tried to be nice,

But the pain of rejection that you felt, after you

Tried once and tried twice, made the third time

Seem like an atrocity.

And, your anger and emotions become aroused

To such a high velocity, that you lose control

And can't help but to react with extreme

Vengeance and force.

The hardest feeling to feel, is the feeling of rejection,

Especially when you give your all to be accepted.

It creates an overwhelming mindset

That makes you feel like you have nothing more

That you can give. "So why live, when it's clear, I'm not

Here, for a purpose that I can fulfill?"

It's unreal, then again, it's all too much the same,

And it constantly runs through my mind on who's to blame.

Is it God's fault? If not, should I call on His name?

And, if so, then from His ways should I refrain?

And go on through life doing my own thing?

Well that's a choice we have to make when

Experiencing pain, because it can make

Or break you, but at the end of the day,

It's our choice to be hateful or let LOVE remain.

No one else can make it for you.

The circumstances can attempt to persuade

your decision, But ultimately

The fate of your decision, will determine and

Create the type of life, you will from that point on, be living.

Will you live with a hateful heart that spreads

More hate in the world?

Or, will you be loving and forgiving,

While living in this hateful world?

Will you choose death and not life,

Because of all the pain and strife?

Or will you choose life and not death?

Because you know, you can

Dust yourself off, puff up your chest

And create change with your very next breath.

Pain is for everybody, experiencing it, is inevitable

To life and that won't change.

It's an unwanted response to a want, need, or desire;

How you choose to deal with it,

can add fuel to the fire, or can be the source

to cease the flames.

Either choice, I understand and can explain,

But for the sake of ending this epidemic

Caused by pain! I would instruct, advise,

Beg, plead and insist, that you resist,

Choosing hate and let LOVE remain;

Because pain is for everybody,

And so, everybody needs change.

VOWS TO LOVE

I Give You Me.... I Do

Today is the day that I accept you as my wife.

Taking full notice of my decision to be your husband,

I give you me, my time, my full commitment, Everything, my life!

I now devote all into you and my seeds which you will one day bare.

And I vow to love, honor, cherish, protect and care for you forever.

Leaving you never, loving you better than I ever have before.

Promising to guide you with God's wisdom, as He opens every door.

I pray for your strength and good health, but should you ever fall ill,

I vow to love you still and always be by your side.

I also pray that our finances never fall short, but whether rich or poor

I vow to love you in the midst.

Knowing this, that if considered poor, I'll work hard until we're rich,

And when rich, I will work hard to keep you happy,

Content and forever in a bliss, from the love I shall give.

I pray for nothing but good days, but should there ever be

Bad days, anger, and pain;

I vow to love you regardless, no matter the circumstances,

I vow to always LetLOVERemain!

I accept you for who you are and I vow to be around and assist

You, as You continue to evolve and grow.

I support your every goal and dream, and I vow to protect

You from any harm, that you may or may not see, or know.

I humbly accept my role as a symbol of how Christ loved the Church.

And, I vow to uphold you, respect you, so that you can remain pure

And unspotted, while receiving the love you deserve.

All this I profess as my devotion, my vows, my truth

And with honor, I accept you as my one and only wife, forever and always...

I Do!